In the Bedi ancestry
Nanak the King was revealed,
He gives pleasure & support to His Sikhs
Wherever they reside.

(Sri Dasam Granth Sahib, 126)

akaal
publishers

© Akaal Publishers 2009

First Published 2009

Third Edition May 2018

Cover Design by www.sikhroots.com

British Library Cataloguing in Publication Data
A catalogue record for this book is available from the British Library

ISBN 978-0-9554587-9-8

Akaal Publishers is a not for profit publisher which publishes books with timeless messages, based upon Sikh history, ethics and philosophy. For further information see our website: www.akaalpublishers.com

The Great Guru Nanak

Vol 1

Translated by, Amanpreet Kaur

Contents

Foreword

This book is the first volume of a set of 4 books, that has been previously published by Damdami Taksal (www.damdamitaksal.com), called Dharam Pothis. Akaal Publishers feels privileged to have been blessed to make this translation from the original Punjabi version into English. It has been done to spread the message of Sri Guru Nanak Dev Jee further afield. This is the first volume of a set of two that will be purely dedicated to Sri Guru Nanak Dev Jee. We will endeavour to get the second volume translated and published as soon as we can.

Our first note of gratitude is to the Great Guru Nanak, whose life and teachings, give us hope and inspiration in a world full of misery and pain. Secondly we would like to thank Bhai Gurdial Singh "Madho Jee" who diligently authored the Dharam Pothis – He likes to remain anonymous, but the grace of Guru Nanak has truly been showered upon him, for he has excellently narrated the life and teachings of Guru Nanak. Gratitude is also expressed to Iqbal Qaiser who has kindly allowed us to reproduce photographs of Nanakan Sahib Gurdwaras from his book, "Historical Sikh Shrines in Pakistan." We would like to thank the design team at www.kalexiko.com for designing the book.

We are sorry for any inaccuracies in translation and welcome readers comments and feedback. Throughout the book we have tried to be as respectful to Sri Guru Nanak Dev Jee as possible, this has been reflected by the fact that we break rules of English grammar, whereby when referring to Guru Jee we have always tried to use capital letters for "He" and so forth. We may have also made the use of capital letters in mid-sentence to add emphasis to certain phrases of Sikh significance.

The book has been translated by Amanpreet Kaur, but I take personal responsibility for any errors or omissions as I conducted the final proofing. We hope readers find our humble effort of value.

Harjinder Singh
Chair, Akaal Publishers
July 2010

Chapter 1
THE GURU AND THE SIKHS

TEACHER:
Children! Can you tell me who Sri Guru Nanak Dev Jee was?

1st CHILD:
Yes! Who doesn't know who Sri Guru Nanak Dev Jee was, they are the first Guru of the Sikhs.

2nd CHILD:
But who is called a Guru?

TEACHER:
Usually any person who teaches us about God and good virtues is called a Guru. However in Sikhi (the Sikh faith), the 10 Guru's from Sri Guru Nanak Dev Jee up to Sri Guru Gobind Singh Jee are seen as our Guru, and all 10 Guru's are accepted as being the same spirit/soul as Sri Guru Nanak Dev Jee.

CHILD:
Guru Jee has now gone back to Sachkhand (Region of Truth). So who is the Sikh's Guru now?

TEACHER:
The present Sikh Guru is Sri Guru Granth Sahib Jee. On 8th October 1708 at Hazoor Sahib (Nanded) Sri Guru Gobind Singh Jee gathered Five Singhs' (initiated Sikhs) in the presence of Sri Guru Granth Sahib Jee and bestowed the Guruship to Sri Guru Granth Sahib Jee. They then commanded that all Sikhs are to believe in Sri Guru Granth Sahib Jee as their living Guru. This is why Sri Guru Granth Sahib Jee is now referred to as the light and spirit, or living

Gurdwara Ramsar Sahib
This is the revered site of where Sri Guru Granth Sahib Jee was
scribed in 1604

form of the Ten Gurus.

CHILDREN:
Sir! Who compiled Sri Guru Granth Sahib Jee?

TEACHER:
Children, Sri Guru Arjan Dev Jee dictated Gurbani (the Guru's word) to Bhai Gurdas Jee at Ramsar Gurdwara (Amritsar) who then scribed Sri Guru Granth Sahib Jee. On the 16th August 1604 at Harmandar Sahib/Golden Temple the first ever installing of Sri Guru Granth Sahib Jee upon a throne took place.

CHILD:
Sir! Please tell us the names of the Ten Gurus?

TEACHER:
Children! Sikhs also refer to their Gurus as Paatshaahiya in the plural or Paatshah in the singular, Paatshah means Eternal King. The Ten Gurus names are as follows:

First Paatshah Sri Guru Nanak Dev Jee
Second Paatshah Sri Guru Angad Dev Jee
Third Paatshah Sri Guru Amar Das Jee
Forth Paatshah Sri Guru Ram Das Jee
Fifth Paatshah Sri Guru Arjan Dev Jee
Sixth Paatshah Sri Guru HarGobind Sahib Jee
Seventh Paatshah Sri Guru HarRai Sahib Jee
Eighth Paatshah Sri Guru HarKrishan Sahib Jee
Ninth Paatshah Sri Guru Tegh Bahadur Sahib Jee
Tenth Paatshah Sri Guru Gobind Singh Jee

The eternal embodiment of the Ten Gurus is Sri Guru Granth Sahib Jee

Harmander Sahib/Golden Temple
The first parkash (enthroning) of Sri Guru Granth Sahib Jee took place here.

CHILD:
Who is called a Sikh?

TEACHER:
A person who lives by and practices the teachings of the
Ten Gurus and Sri Guru Granth Sahib Jee. They do not follow any
other religion, they are known as Sikhs. But children, may I also
ask a question now?

CHILDREN:
Sure! Please do.

TEACHER:
Tell me how can a Sikh be recognized? How can you tell by looking
at someone that they are a Sikh and not from some other religion?

CHILDREN:
Well that's obvious! A Sikh has uncut hair on their head and the
men have an unshaven/uncut beard on their face. That's how to
recognize a Sikh.

TEACHER:
That's correct, but there are also other distinctive features of a Sikh
other than their uncut hair and beards, tell me what these are?

CHILD:
Yes! Sikhs keep a wooden comb(Kanga) in their hair. They wear an
iron bangle (Kara) on their wrist, they wear white shorts (Kachera)
and also wear a small sword (Kirpaan).

TEACHER:
You are all very wise! So the five distinguishing features of a Sikh
are:

(1) Kesh - beard and/or uncut hair

(2) Kanga - wooden comb

(3) Kara - iron bangle

(4) Kachera - white shorts

(5) Kirpaan - small sword

All these five words in Gurmukhi script begin with the letter 'K', that's why they are called the Five K's or 'Kakaar'. It is very important for every Sikh to carry and have these five K's on their bodies at all times.

REVISION QUESTIONS
CHAPTER 1

1. Who is called a Guru?
2. Which Guru had Sri Guru Granth Sahib Jee scribed and where was this done?
3. When was Sri Guru Granth Sahib Jee 'enthroned' or installed at Harmandar Sahib?
4. Learn the names of the Gurus and tell me them?
5. Who is the present Sikh Guru?
6. Who is called a Sikh and what are the distinguishing features of Sikhs?

Chapter 2
SRI GURU NANAK DEV JEE'S CHILDHOOD(BAAL-LILA)

Sri Guru Nanak Dev Jee was born in Rai Bhoi Dee Talvandi on 20th October 1469 AD. This birth place is now in Pakistan, Dist: Shekhupura. After Sri Guru Nanak Dev Jee was born Rai Bular who was the Governore of the area, changed the name of the village from Rai Bhoe Dee Talvandi to Nankana Sahib.

Guru Jee's fathers name was Mehta Kalyan Chand Jee. He was normally referred to as Mehta Kalu. Guru Jee's mother's name was Mata Tripta Jee. Guru Jee also had one sister, she was five years older than Guru Jee, her name was Bebe Nanaki. Guru Jee's paternal uncle's name was Lal Chand Jee. Guru Jee's paternal family village was Dera Sahib (Patthay Vind), which is in the district of Amritsar at a distance of about 20km from Tarn Taaran Sahib. Their maternal family village was Dehra Chahal which is (in between Lahore and Ghavindi) about 35km from Lahore as you are travelling towards Ghavindi.

Bebe Nanaki was born in their maternal family's village (Dehra Chahal). As Guru Jee's maternal family were all living here they visited this village frequently. Guru Jee's maternal grandfather was Bhai Rama Jee, their maternal grandmother was Bhiraaee Jee and maternal uncle was Krishan Jee.

When Guru Jee was about five years old they would play with children of their age and quite often would talk about the greatness of God. The other children would listen to these sermons with great love and interest and would always remain in the company of Guru Jee. Even people passing by that would hear Guru Jee's sweet words, would say that this child is speaking with the wisdom

Gurdwara Janam Asthan, Nanakana Sahib
Birth place of Sri Guru Nanak Dev Jee

of an enlightened soul.

When Guru Jee was of school age their father first sent them to Gopaal Dhat Pandit (a Hindu Scholar) to study. Guru Jee continued to study with this teacher for about two days. On the third day Guru Jee recited some Bani (hymns) which surprised the teacher. The Pandit said to Baba Kalu Jee, your son already knows everything I could teach him, He does not need to learn anything from me, He is an enlightened soul. Then Guru Jee's father sent Guru Jee to Noor Deen Mulla (a Muslim Priest/Scholar) to learn 'Farsi'(Persian). After two days Guru Jee again recited Bani/hymns in Farsi to the Mullla and surprised him also. Hence Guru Jee's childhood traits were extraordinary. This was the childhood of Guru Jee.

Guru Jee was an ocean of mercy. Whenever He saw any poor, helpless, less fortunate or hungry person. He would always give something to them. Guru Jee would always meditate on God's name and also encourage their friends and companions to also meditate.

After some time Guru Jee started to live in a state of being detached from the world, not taking an interest in the world at all. Seeing this, people started to say things like 'Guru Jee has a curse.' Some people would say Guru Jee has been possessed. These foolish people did not know the greatness of Guru Jee. Some time passed in this way.

Baba Kalu Jee thought *'my son is bored and sad, I should get him to start doing some work'* after thinking about this for some time Baba Kalu Jee said to Guru Jee, *"our servants do not look after our cattle very well. From tomorrow morning I want you to look after the cattle whilst they graze."*

Guru Jee replied, *"Sure Father, as of tomorrow I will graze the cattle and look after them."* The next day at sunrise Guru Jee took

Gurdwara Patti Sahib (near Nanakana Sahib)
This is where Guru Nanak taught the Pandit

the cattle out to graze. All day the cattle grazed in the fields and in the evening Guru Jee returned home with the cattle. Baba Kalu Jee was very pleased after seeing this.

Guru Jee continued taking cattle out to graze everyday, thereafter. Then one day Guru Jee felt tired and lay down to rest. While Guru Jee was sleeping, the cattle entered a field of corn and ruined all the corn by grazing there. The farmer who owned the field of corn arrived there and he was horrified and shocked at what he saw in his field, all his crops had been ruined by the cattle in the field.

The farmer said out loud, *"Which lazy person has allowed the cattle to ruin my field?"* On hearing this Guru Jee awoke and quickly started to move the cattle out of the field. The farmer said *"you must pay for the damage your cattle have done to my field or I am going to tell Rai Bular."* Rai Bular was the governor of the area, he was the leader of the local administration of the government of the day.

Shouting at Guru Jee the farmer went to complain and said to Rai Bular, *"your octoroon's (patvari's) son has ruined all my crops. Please get me justice."* After hearing this Rai Bular called Baba Kalu Jee and said *"your son is a dreamer, why do you send him to graze cattle?"* After hearing these words Guru Jee said, *"the cattle have not done any damage to the field. The field is just as green and full of crops as it was before."* The farmer said *"He has ruined all my crops."*

Rai Bular sent one of his men to go and look at the field to check what state it was in. Just as Guru Jee had said the field was full of healthy green crops. After seeing the field full of crops that appeared to be very green and healthy, the man returned and said this farmer is telling lies.

Gurdwara Kiara Sahib (near Nanakana Sahib)
Marks the site of the field that was ruined and replenished

On hearing this, the farmer went to look at the field for himself. Seeing his field full of healthy crops he was shocked, and feeling very embarrassed he returned to Rai Bular. Rai Bular knew the farmer had lied. It was the farmers bad luck that even on seeing this miracle Guru Jee had done, he could still not bow down before Guru Jee and recognize Guru Jee's true identity. Baba Kalu Jee and Guru Jee went back home. There is now a Gurdwara called Kiaara Sahib at this historic and blessed place of this field.

REVISION QUESTIONS
CHAPTER 2

1. Where and when was Guru Jee born?
2. What were the names of Guru Jee's father, mother and sister?
3. Who did Baba Kalu Jee send Guru Jee to study from first?
4. When Guru Jee started to live in a state of being detached from the world, what did people say about him?
5. Can you tell me the story of the field which got replenished with crops?

Chapter 3
THE COBRA PROVIDED SHADE FOR GURU JEE

It was the month of Vaisakh (April/May) and Guru Jee was in the forest grazing cattle. In the afternoon it was very hot, Guru Jee put down a sheet under the shade of a very large tree and lay down to sleep. After some time the sun got even brighter and hotter, as the day went by the shade from the tree moved to another side.

Sheshnag (the king of the snakes) saw this and thought I must serve Guru Jee by providing shade from the very bright sunlight. After thinking about serving Guru Jee Shehshnag took the form of a white cobra and came and bowed at Guru Jee's feet and did three parkarma or walked around Guru Jee (this is done as a mark of respect to say Guru Jee is bigger and better than him and is done as a humbling process). The cobra then went round to Guru Jee's head and fanned his hood to provide shade for Guru Jee from the sunlight. A lot of time passed with the cobra shading Guru Jee from the sun, while He slept.

The governor of Talvandi, Rai Bular was on his way back to Talvandi with his army. He was very fortunate, as he saw the cobra and he went a little closer. He thought either the snake has killed the child, and if the child is alive he surely must be a holy person of God and the snake is serving Him by providing shade from the blazing sun, whilst He sleeps. The governor sent one of his servants to have a closer look.

At seeing the approaching servant the snake quickly went away. The governor then got onto his horse and went a little closer to see for himself. There were a lot of warriors with him.

The governor was amazed by what he saw. He got off his horse and bowed down at the feet of Guru Jee, who is the destroyer of all evil deeds. From that day onwards the governor recognized Guru Jee as a messenger of God and never doubted this. The governor then got back onto his horse and returned to his village with his army. He thought, 'when this child grows up I will request him to grant me immortality.'

The governor sent a servant to call Baba Kalu Jee. Upon arrival he respectfully sat Baba Kalu by his side and said, *"Kalyan Chand! Stop thinking of your son as your own, he is God himself that has come to your house in this human form of your son. You must have done some very good deeds in your past lives to be so fortunate. I don't know anyone as fortunate as you. Keep serving your son lovingly with clothes and food. Don't ever disrespect Guru Jee. Always be loyal and respectful to him as he is truly the reflection of God."* Rai Bular then told Baba Kalu Jee about the whole incident of the cobra that served Guru Jee. *"He was sleeping under a tree and as the direct sunlight was hitting his face the snake fanned its hood to provide shade so as to allow Guru Jee to have a peaceful sleep. On seeing us approaching the snake quickly went away,"* said Rai Bular.

On hearing this Baba Kalu Jee said that's great. Baba Kalu was greedy for money and wealth and thought, 'all the wealth is in Guru Jee's command and can be utilised in whichever way Guru Jee wishes.' Baba Kalu Jee returned home happily. Guru Jee happily returned home with the cattle. From that day onwards the villagers of Talvandi started to sing the praises of Guru Jee. They were all saying Kalu Jee's son has great powers. A snake shaded him from the blazing sunlight and Rai Bular witnessed this. This child is hiding His greatness and powers from everyone and does not show them off.

REVISION QUESTIONS
CHAPTER 3

1. Why did Sheshnag serve Guru Jee? What did he believe Guru Jee was?
2. Why did Rai Bular believe that Guru Jee was the form of God?
3. What was Rai Bular thinking about the future?
4. What did Rai Bular say to Baba Kalu Jee about Guru Jee?
5. After hearing about Guru Jee and what Rai Bular Jee witnessed, what were the people of the village saying about Guru Jee?

Chapter 4
WHILE FARMING, GURU JEE HALTS THE SHADE OF A TREE

One day Baba Kalu Jee lovingly said to Guru Jee, *"Son you are quite mature now. Instead of grazing cattle why don't you go to the cattle market and buy two strong bulls and start farming in our fields. Water the crops and keep them safe from animals. Then when the crops have grown, gather them and sell them at the market. If you produce a lot of crops I will employ more servants to help you. We will have endless amounts of food and money in our home this way."* Guru Jee replied, *"as you wish Father. I will do just as you want me to."* Baba Kalu Jee gave Guru Jee some seeds from home and sent a servant with him to help. The two of them took the seeds and started to plough the fields and sow the seeds. After ploughing the whole field and sowing all the seeds the two of them returned home. Baba Kalu Jee was very pleased.

Guru Jee was very blessed and on the third day, all the crops had started to grow and the whole of the field was full of growing green crops. This pleased Baba Kalu Jee a lot and he started to think about what a great farmer his son was and how they would soon be very rich. I will give him a separate village and he will earn a very good living. For some time Baba Kalu Jee carried on thinking about this. Guru Jee realised that his father's greed for wealth was growing day by day and felt that He had to put a stop to it soon.

Daily, Guru Jee would go to the field to do the farming and look after the crops. He would never stop any cattle or animals entering the field or eating and destroying the crops. Guru Jee allowed the cattle to do as they pleased. One day when Baba Kalu Jee Jee went to check on the farming he saw Guru Jee sitting nearby and not stopping any cattle from eating the crops. On seeing this Baba

Kalu Jee Jee was very angry and in his rage he said some very nasty things like, *"I have such bad luck, ever since you have been born into my family, you have ruined my house. You haven't changed these bad habits of yours since childhood. You have given away all our possessions and have wasted the wealth of our house. Now you are of the age to earn a living, and instead you are making silly errors. How will you earn a living to feed yourself when I am no longer here? You will probably leave home one day with the holy men (Fakirs)?* After saying nasty things like this Baba Kalu Jee Jee returned home. From that day onwards Guru Jee started to remain very sad and detached. Some people talked about how powerful Guru Jee was. During the day Guru Jee would go out of the village and sit under the shade of a large tree. He spent a lot of time there alone, and didn't speak to anyone.

One afternoon Guru Jee put down a sheet and lay down to sleep under the cool shade of a large tree. A short while later Rai Bular and his men were on their travels and came past the area where Guru Jee was resting. Rai Bular went and stood by Guru Jee and to his amazement he couldn't believe his eyes. He said to his men, *"Look at this amazing miracle, the shade from all the trees in the area have changed direction as the day has gone on and the sun has changed direction. However the large tree under which Kalu's son is sleeping still has it's shade covering him unlike the others which have all changed direction. He truly is a very blessed and Godly person, whoever shall serve him, will be liberated from the cycle of births and deaths."* This is the second time that I have witnessed such a miracle. On saying this Rai Bular put both his hands together and bowed down on the floor before Guru Jee. He then returned to his village.

REVISION QUESTIONS
CHAPTER 4

1. Why did Baba Kalu Jee Jee stop Guru Jee grazing cattle and what did he say to Guru Jee?
2. What did Guru Jee do to the green crops and why?
3. Why did Guru Jee start to feel sad and detached?
4. When Guru Jee was sleeping under the shade of the tree what miraculous thing did Rai Bular see?

Chapter 5

GURU JEE & A TRUE TRADE

When Guru Jee was about 15-16 years old Baba Kalu Jee explained to Guru Jee, *"You are our only son and you should start to earn a living, without working and earning money, the household cannot be run."* Guru Jee said, *"Father, please forgive me for my past mistakes. I will now do just as you please."*

Baba Kalu Jee thought about getting his son into business and said, *"Son, take twenty rupees and go and start trading to make a profit."* Baba Jee meant for Guru Jee to go to a different town or market, to buy some genuine goods and then to go to a different town or market, and sell them at a higher price in order to make a profit. In this way Guru Jee will build on the profit and will multiply this amount by many times. Baba Kalu Jee Jee called Bhai Bala and said *"Bala, go with Nanak and invest the money into purchasing genuine profitable goods that you find."* After saying this Baba Kalu Jee Jee handed twenty rupees to Bhai Bala.

Obeying his father's orders Guru Jee left with Bhai Bala. Some 15km from their village they came across a jungle near a village called Churkanai. Guru Jee noticed a dera (abode) of Saadhus (holy men). There were lots of these holy men in deep meditation, they were meditating to achieve liberation. The Mahant (leader of these holy men) was sitting on a higher platform and reciting God's name. On seeing this Guru Jee stood up and said to Bhai Bala, *"I feel this is a needy cause and don't feel like looking any further for a place to spend the money. Father said to invest the money on a profitable cause to do a true deal, and I can't think of a more profitable cause to spend the money on. Let's give the money to these holy men. They can buy food with the money."*

On hearing this Bhai Bala Jee said, *"I'm scared of Baba Kalu Jee Jee's temper. I will leave this for you to tell your Father and sort out with him. I am your friend and I will not disagree with you on this matter. Do as you feel is best."* Bhai Bala then handed the 20 rupees to Guru Jee.

Guru Jee went up to the Mahant (leader of the Sadhus), bowed down respectfully in front of him and sat down. He asked the Mahant, *"Do you eat food, or just meditate all day and night on an empty stomach?"* The Mahant replied, *"to achieve liberation we have adorned the attire of saadhus (holy men). When it comes to food, we eat whatever is donated to us and are content with this."*

Guru Jee was pleased by what He heard and went on to ask the Mahant, *"What is your name?"* the Mahant replied, *"My name is Santren (meaning, living a saintly life)."* Guru Jee was even happier on hearing his name and placed the 20 rupees in front of the Mahant and said, *"buy food to eat with this money. I know all about your ways now. You do not beg or ask anyone for anything. Whatever anyone donates to you, you happily receive and eat. God has sent this money for you. Ensure that you all enjoy the food and produce bought with it."* The Mahant then said to Guru Jee, *"You are very young, all your dealings are to be done according to your Father's wishes. What work has your Father sent you to do? If you go home empty handed your Father will throw you out."*

Guru Jee said, *"Sant Jee, it is my father's wish that I invest this money into a profitable cause. Hence I can't think of a more profitable cause, this is definitely the best place to invest the money."* On hearing this the mahant said *"If this is how you feel, take the money and go and buy food for everyone."* Guru Jee took the money and bought lots of food from the city with it. On returning they placed all the food in front of the mahant and sat down. Guru Jee asked the mahant, *"If you allow, may we prepare the food for you, then all*

Gurdwara Sacha Sauda
Where the true trade was conducted

the saints can eat together." The mahant replied, *"The saints will prepare their own food and eat it, you go back home to your village now."* Guru Jee and Bhai Bala returned home to Talvandi. At the place where this true trade was done now stands a Gurdwara named *"Sacha Saudha"* (true trade).

This is the first historical example of Langar or a free kitchen being set up in Sikhi. The Sadhus were given Langar by Guru Jee and this true trade of 20 Rupees has led to Langar being served in Gurdwaras throughout the globe.

REVISION QUESTIONS
CHAPTER 5

1. Why did Baba Kalu Jee give Guru Jee 20 rupees?
2. Who did Guru Jee go with, to do a true trade?
3. What type of trading did Guru Jee do?
4. What did the mahant of the saadhus say to Guru Jee?
5. What reply did Guru Jee give to the mahant?

Chapter 6
GURU JEE RETURNS HOME AFTER DOING THE TRUE TRADE

When Guru Jee was returning home He came close to Talvandi and thought, Father will not agree that I have done a good thing. He will say I have wasted the money. He will definitely be angry. Outside the village, there was a tree. Its branches were large and bending over to touch the floor. It looked like a tent. Guru Jee sat below this tree and told Bhai Bala to go home. Bhai Bala obeyed Guru Jee and went home.

When Baba Kalu Jee came to know that Bhai Bala had returned home alone, he sent a servant to call Bhai Bala. Bhai Bala told Baba Kalu Jee everything. After hearing this Baba Kalu Jee entered a rage. He went to where Guru Jee was sitting under the tree and started to slap him. Mata Tripta sent Bebe Nanaki to save Guru Jee from the rage of their Father. Some of the villagers also gathered there to see what was happening. Baba Kalu Jee was hitting Guru Jee and Bebe Nanaki Jee intervened and managed to save Guru Jee from him. The villagers that had gathered there also tried to convince Baba Kalu Jee to calm down and stop hitting Guru Jee. They all took Guru Jee home.

On seeing Guru Jee, Mata Tripta embraced him in her arms and said, *"Son! From now on don't do any work. If you don't do any work there will be no arguments. God has blessed our home with everything we could ever need."*

One of the villagers that had witnessed everything went to Rai Bular and told him what he had seen and heard. On hearing this Rai Bular sent a servant to go and call Guru Jee and Baba Kalu Jee. When Guru Jee arrived, Rai Bular got up from his throne and respectfully requested Guru Jee to sit next to him. Rai Bular started to say to Baba Kalu Jee, *"Kalu, you are a very conniving and a bad hearted man, you only think of wealth and getting richer and are very greedy. You have not listened to even one thing I have said to you. You have not recognized the true identity and Godly qualities or special powers of this blessed son of yours."*

Baba Kalu Jee said, *"you are always getting angry at me. Think in your mind with a clear head, who is actually at fault here? I gave him money to do business with. He gave all the money to the holy men and then on returning home sat and hid outside the village under a tree. He did not come home and tell me what He had done. Bala told me everything that had happened."* Rai Bular said, *"you have a heart of stone, you do not know the greatness of your son."* At this point Rai Bular had 20 rupees bought from his safe and gave them to Baba Kalu Jee.

Baba Kalu Jee said, *"Governor, I am not just angry about the 20 rupees He has thrown away, as He is always irresponsible. I am just worried about how He will manage the household once I have gone. These rupees you are giving me and all the wealth that I own, is all due to your kindness. It is only due to your generosity that I have everything in my home."* Rai Bular gave Baba Kalu the 20 rupees but Baba Kalu Jee was not accepting them. Then one of the governor's men said, *"you should not disobey the order of an elder. Accept the rupees the governor is giving you and in future don't ever shout or tell you son off again."*

After insisting, Rai Bular managed to give Baba Kalu Jee the rupees. Baba Kalu Jee returned home feeling very embarrassed. The villagers started to gossip and spread rumours about how bad Baba Kalu Jee was.

Very soon Baba Kalu Jee heard these rumors, He was very hurt and did not know what to say in his defense. After paying some thought to this, Baba Kalu Jee returned to Rai Bular with the rupees and said, *"Governor, take your money back, people in the village are saying very nasty and hurtful things about me. I can't keep hearing all this talk."*

The governor said, *"eradicate the anger out of your mind. I have borrowed this money off them (Guru Jee) and given it to you, take it home. Don't ever get angry at Guru Jee again."* Baba Kalu Jee was surprised and said, *"He has never earned even a single penny. How could He possibly have loaned you the money. if He earned money there wouldn't have been such a commotion in the first place."* Rai Bular said, *"Kalu! All the wealth you see around you, belongs to Guru Jee and is within his control."* Rai Bular hence explained to Baba Kalu how everything he owned belonged to Guru Jee. Baba Kalu Jee then returned home.

REVISION QUESTIONS
CHAPTER 6

1. Why did Guru Jee not return home after doing the true trade?
2. When Baba Kalu Jee was slapping Guru Jee who came to save Guru Jee?
3. When Baba Kalu Jee went to return the 20 rupees to Rai Bular what did Rai Bular say?
4. Who did Rai Bular say he had borrowed the money from?

Chapter 7
GURU JEE GOES TO SULTANPUR LODH

Bebe Nanaki was married in Sultanpur Lodhi Lodhi (Dist. Kapurthla) to Jai Ram the son of Parmanand Jee. Jai Ram came from Sultanpur Lodhi to his in-laws home in Talvandi, to Baba Kalu Jee's house to take Bebe Nanaki home. When Rai Bular heard of Jai Ram's arrival, he at once sent a servant to go and call Jai Ram. Rai Bular told Jai Ram Jee all about Guru Jee. *"He is the true form of God. He has many virtues and powers and can perform miracles. Kalu Jee does not know or recognize this. He is forever arguing and fighting with Guru Jee. When you return to your home, I will send them (Guru Jee) to you. Serve them with love and receive their blessings and happiness."*

Jai Ram was very happy after hearing all this. He said, *"when they come to our home we will truly be very blessed."* Jai Ram bid farewell to Rai Bular and after staying at his in-laws house for a few days returned to Sultanpur Lodhi with Bebe Nanaki Jee.

Some time passed by. Rai Bular was very hurt and upset by Baba Kalu Jee's bad treatment of Guru Jee. He sent a servant to go and call Guru Jee and said to Guru Jee, *"go to your sister's home. I will write a letter to Jai Ram. I will be able to live with peace of mind if you go and stay there. Here Baba Kalu Jee fights and argues with you on a daily basis."* Rai Bular then wrote a letter to Jai Ram. Guru Jee went home and got his mother's blessings and permission to go to Sultanpur Lodhi, He then bowed down at Mata Tripta Jee's feet. Guru Jee also went with both hands clapsed and bowed down respectfully before His Father.

Guru Jee also went to bid farewell to all His childhood friends and companions. Then accompanied with Bhai Bala Jee and everyone's blessings Guru Jee left for Sultanpur Lodhi.

On reaching Sultanpur Lodhi Guru Jee went to Jai Ram's house and when His sister Bebe Nanaki saw Guru Jee, she came running and bowed down before Guru Jee. On seeing this Guru Jee said, *"it is not right for you to do this, you have done the opposite to what is expected."* Bebe Nanaki Jee replied, *"I do not think of you as my younger brother, I only know you as being the true form of God. You have taken on this human form at your wish, to help destroy evil and ignorance in the world. You have come to earth to dispel the hatred and sin that dwells within people in this dark age (Kaljug)."*

In this time, Jai Ram arrived and stepped forward to greet Guru Jee. Guru Jee said to Jai Ram, *"You are my elder"* and then stepped forward to respectfully greet Jai Ram. Jai Ram said, *"I have always awaited your arrival. By finally setting foot in our home you have blessed us. I will be content and fulfilled by doing your service and keeping your company."*

In this way the two of them were very happy to meet one another. Jai Ram started to serve Guru Jee with great love and devotion and always remained in Guru Jee's company. Guru Jee remained in Sultanpur for some time.

One day Guru Jee said to Bebe Nanaki Jee, *"Sister, it is not right for me to stay here and sit idle. Let me do a job so that my mind remains engaged,"* to which His sister replied *"You are the ruler of the world. Do as you wish. You talk about spirituality and meditating on God with the holy men. It does not suit you to do a regular job. Sit at home and bless us with divine hymns and praises of the almighty Lord."* Guru Jee replied, *"Sister, please listen. Even the Vedas state that we should earn an honest living with our own hands, in order to live and feed ourselves. We should also donate part of our earnings to the poor and needy."*

Jai Ram then said, *"I respect your wishes. I cannot disobey or ignore your request. If you can do accounting work we can get you a job as an account keeper."* Guru Jee said, *"I know all about account keeping, paying for our mistakes and giving and taking."*

REVISION QUESTIONS
CHAPTER 7

1. Where and with whom did Bebe Nanaki's marriage take place?
2. What did Rai Bular say to Jai Ram about Guru Jee?
3. Why did Rai Bular send Guru Jee to Sultanpur?
4. When Bebe Nanaki bowed down before Guru Jee. What did Guru Jee say and what was Bebe Nanaki's reply?
5. What did Guru Jee say was stated in the Vedas?

GURU JEE WORKS AS A STOREKEEPER

Jai Ram said to Guru Jee, *"If you can do the job of a storekeeper I can speak to the governor Daulat Khan and get you employed as a storekeeper. This is a good job."* Guru Jee agreed with Jai Ram and said, *"God himself will help me do this job to the best of my ability."* Jai Ram said *"Let's meet Daulat Khan today and sort it out."* Jai Ram and Guru Jee went to see the governor about the job of storekeeper. Daulat Khan looked at Guru Jee and said He can do the job of a storekeeper and happily gave Guru Jee a uniform and also 1000 rupees to start the job as a storekeeper.

Guru Jee bought rations from the market and put them into the store. From morning till night, the store was very busy with wholesalers who would come and buy rations.

One day Bhai Bala Jee said to Guru Jee, *"please allow me to leave. I will go home and earn a living as a farmer."* Guru Jee said, *"Bala, stay here and meditate on God's name and earn an honest living, don't be sad or home sick. Don't go like this, we will earn a lot of wealth by working hard as storekeepers. We must stay here for some time. Then we must go to some other place. I will take you with me."* In this way Guru Jee lovingly convinced Bhai Bala to stay with him.

Bhai Bala said, *"Guru Jee! Please give me your blessings so that I may never disobey your orders. May I always listen to you."* Guru Jee said, *"you are my friend, your mind will always remain attached to God."* Bhai Bala on hearing these words bowed down respectfully at Guru Jee's feet. From that day onwards Bhai Bala remained with Guru Jee and always served them. Hearing about

Guru Jee's greatness many people came to beg for rations from Guru Jee. Whoever came to Guru Jee, had their wishes granted, and were never turned away empty handed. Guru Jee gave everyone whatever they asked for and the store was never short of anything. In this way, in every home, people started to sing the praises of Guru Jee.

Every month the accounts of the store were checked and read to the governor. Every time the accounts were read out Guru Jee had always made a profit. Some idle gossipers were jealous of Guru Jee's success, and said the governor doesn't know that his storekeeper is robbing his store. In the end he will lose out on everything and become bankrupt. The governor will then arrest Him. He will be very hurt. Some say He gives away too much as charity, hence a lot of rations are wasted and lost in this way.

In Talvandi Baba Kalu heard of the many praises people were singing of Guru Jee. He came from Talvandi to Sultanpur Lodhi. When Guru Jee saw Baba Kalu, He quickly got up and greeted His Father by bowing respectfully at Baba Kalu's feet. Baba Kalu met Guru Jee with lots of love and happiness. Bhai Bala then also bowed at Baba Kalu 's feet and greeted him and asked how everyone was.
After a short while Baba Kalu Jee said, *"Son, you have been doing the job of a storekeeper for quite some time now. How much money have you earned? Give it to me."* Guru Jee said, *"I have earned a lot but I receive money with the one hand and it is spent with the other. I have not saved a penny. My earnings and outgoings are equal."*

Baba Kalu Jee was very angry upon hearing this. He said, *"You do not look after your wealth. You have been doing this job for so long and haven't saved a single penny!"* Baba Kalu Jee was also very angry at Bhai Bala and said, *"You stay with him, even you didn't look after the money you earned."* After saying some very nasty

Gurdwara Hatt Sahib (near Nanakana Sahib)
This is where Guru Jee ran his store

things Baba Kalu Jee said, *"I want you to earn and repay all the money of mine that you have wasted. I have come to collect it from you."* On hearing this Guru Jee remained quiet and did not reply. Baba Kalu said, *"Stop spending money on worthless things. Use common sense and save money. If you don't want to give it to me then keep it separately. Households cannot be run without money."* In this way Baba Kalu explained to Guru Jee how he should earn and save money, and then went to Jai Ram's house. On arriving there he met Bebe Nanaki, Jai Ram and their whole family with great love. He stayed with them for some days and then returned to Talvandi.

Just as people purchase rations from government run stores at a lower price and the money earned is deposited into the government treasury nowadays, the same was done in those days at the stores (modhikhana, this is in reference to stores in India). Guru Jee performed the job of storekeeper in a very honest manner. He would always weigh in full or excess, and never short changed anyone, or over-priced goods. Everyone loved Guru Jee, however some bad people went to the governor and said your storekeeper is running your store into the ground and at a loss. On hearing this Guru Jee was imprisoned and all the figures and accounts were checked many times over. The accounts kept showing that Guru Jee had saved extra rations and made a profit.

The governor was then convinced Guru Jee had not cheated the store and released Guru Jee. The slanderous people who had complained about Guru Jee were very ashamed and embarrassed. Guru Jee worked very hard to earn an honest living whilst meditating on God's name and encouraged others to meditate on God's name. Guru Jee often gave food and clothes to the poor and needy from His own earnings. Guru Jee truly lived by the values that He taught.

Stone-weights that Guru Jee used to weigh rations in the store. These are now stored in Gurdwara Hatt Sahib.

Gurdwara Sri Khotri Sahib
Prison cell in which Sri Guru Nanak Dev Jee was imprisoned whilst his accounts were checked.

Guru Jee lived in accordance with the three Golden rules He preached about:

1. Earn an honest living.
2. Meditate on God's name
3. Share a part of your earnings with the poor and needy.

REVISION QUESTIONS
CHAPTER 8

1. What did Daulat Khan say when he saw Guru Jee and what did he give Guru Jee?
2. What blessings did Bhai Bala seek from Guru Jee and what did Guru Jee say?
3. How did Guru Jee conduct himself while doing the job of storekeeper?
4. What did the slanderous people say to the governor about Guru Jee?
5. How many golden rules was Guru Jee living and showing us?

Gurdwara Guru Ka Bagh
Guru Jee's house in Sultanpur Lodhi, Guru Jee's sons Baba Sri Chand & Baba Lakhmi Das were born here.

Chapter 9
BHAGIRATH COMES TO GURU JEE

Near Sultanpur Lodhi in a town called Malseeha lived a devotee of Kalka Devi (goddess) named Bhagirath. Everyday he would go to the Mandir (temple) to worship and serve Kalka Devi with great love and devotion and would sing the Devi's praises. He would pray for Mukti (liberation) day and night.

One day Bhagirath was worshipping at the temple, he became so engrossed in devotional prayers that the whole day passed in this way. Even late in the evening he was just as passionate and sincere as he was in the morning. That night he stayed at the temple. At about midnight he started to feel tired and fell asleep. As he slept, in his dream Kalka Devi appeared and asked, *"Dear follower! Ask for whatever you wish."*

Bhagirath replied, *"Devi Jee! If you are happy with my prayers and offerings, please grant me mukti (liberation)."* The Devi said, *"I cannot grant this wish of yours and give you liberation, if this is what you want then there is a messenger of God living in Sultanpur Lodhi named Sri Guru Nanak Dev Jee. He is working as a storekeeper. Go and worship him with sincere devotion. He is the person who can free you from the cycle of births and deaths."* At this point Bhagirath awoke and started to think about his dream. He decided that he would go to Guru Jee the next morning.

The next morning Bhagirath got ready to go to the True Guru, Sri Guru Nanak Dev Jee, leaving behind his family and position. Many people tried to talk him out of going, but he was determined and left. He arrived at Sultanpur Lodhi and outside the store where Guru Jee worked, he saw a gathering of poor people and beggars. Bhagirath was very anxious and had a longing to meet Guru Jee. On seeing Guru Jee he lay down flat, with his forehead touching the floor, without paying a single thought about his body or clothes. Guru Jee knew everything about the Devi and helped Bhagirath up by holding his arms and said, *"What is your wish and where have you come from? Tell me all about yourself. Whatever you ask for will be granted."* On hearing this Bhagirath said, *"You are an enlightened soul and know everything. Even so on your questioning, I will tell you everything. I live in the town of Malseeha. I am a devotee and follower of Kalka Devi. In my dream Kalka Devi visited me and told me that if I wanted to attain liberation I must go to the True Guru, Sri Guru Nanak Dev Jee and serve him with sincerity and devotion. Hence I have come to serve you."* On hearing this Guru Jee was very pleased and gave him permission to stay and serve Him. In this way Bhagirath served Guru Jee daily and reaped the fruits of his honest devotion and received many blessings.

REVISION QUESTIONS
CHAPTER 9

1. Where did Bhagirath live and who did he worship?
2. What did Kalka Devi say to Bhagirath in his dream?
3. What did Guru Jee say to Bhagirath?

Chapter 10
BHAI MARDANA COMES TO GURU JEE

Bhai Mardana came from Talvandi to Sultanpur Lodhi to meet Guru Jee and obtain His blessings. He respectfully bowed down at Guru Jee's feet and greeted Guru Jee, he passed on the well wishes and messages from the residents of Talvandi. Then Mardana made a request to Guru Jee, *"Guru Jee! You said that I am the bard (Marasi) of the Bedi family and that I should only ask you if I have any unfulfilled needs or wants. Remembering these words of yours I have come to you. Everything is going well. I have set the date for my daughter's wedding and I do not have enough money to carry out the wedding arragements. This is why I have come to you for help."*

At this point Guru Jee said to Bhagirath make a list of all the provisions and expenses to carry out the wedding. Bhagirath sat with Bhai Mardana and compiled a list of all the things needed for the wedding. Guru Jee said, *"We do not have all these things here. Therefore, Bhagirath you must go to Lahore and carefully buy all these things. Do not stay there for longer than one night."* Bhagirath went to complete the shopping in Lahore, the owner of the shop where he stopped was named Mansukh. Bhagirath showed him the list and said, *" Oh storekeeper, please can you arrange to supply me with all the items on this list for a wedding. I will pay you cash in full. I cannot stay here longer than one night."*

The shopkeeper sat Bhagirath down by himself and said, *"It's now evening, I will get you all the stuff on this list by tomorrow."* When the shopkeeper saw all the things written on the list he said, *"You can get everything but it will take some time to get the bridal (ivory) bangles made."* Bhagirath Jee said, *"If I stay here a second night my life will be worthless."* The shopkeeper asked, *"What is the* reason for this? Why do you have to return so quickly? Please put my curiosity to rest." Bhagirath said, "Shopkeeper, my Guru is perfect. His words never go unfulfilled. It is their wish that I not stay a second night in Lahore." Mansukh said, "There is no-one so complete and pure as you describe, in this Kaljug." Bhagirath said, "Do not mock or doubt what I say, my Guru is very enlightened and whoever has had complete faith in Him, has been liberated from the cycle of births and deaths. In Kaljug, God himself has come in this human form. However they live and earn a living, like any other human being. They are all knowing, and know everything about every one's inner thoughts and feelings." Mansukh said, "If they show me some of the miraculous things they can perform, I too will become a Sikh (follower/believer) of theirs. I have met a lot of fake saints, hence without witnessing their miracles with my own eyes I cannot have faith in Him."

Bhagirath Jee said, "Mansukh, discard your criticisms and with true faith, go and obtain the blessings of Guru Jee, with which your mind will be at peace. If it's miracles you want to see, then there are no shortages of miracles there. Set your mind set to believe and come with me, Guru Jee will grant all your wishes and desires." On hearing this Mansukh had the desire to meet Guru Jee. Talking like this, they passed the evening, the two of them had dinner and then went to sleep.

Both of them awoke at the crack of dawn, washed and got ready. Mansukh said to Bhagirath, "I have a servant at my house. I don't feel like paying him yet. I will give the money as an offering to Guru Jee instead." Bhagirath said, "Do as you feel is best"

They packed all the wedding shopping and left to go to Sultanpur Lodhi. Mansukh said to Bhagirath, "If Guru Jee says my name when speaking to me, my faith will be instilled, and I will definitely believe that they are the form of God." The two of them arrived at Sultanpur Lodhi. As Guru Jee saw the two of them approaching He said, *"Come oh benevolent Bhagirath. This Mansukh was a non-believer before. Now he wishes to obtain true happiness of mind just as is suggested in the meaning of his name –Mansukh (mind of happiness)."* On hearing these words Mansukh lay down flat at the feet of Guru Jee. Bhagirath put all the purchased items for the wedding in front of Guru Jee, respectfully bowed down and said, *"You know everything, he has come to become a Sikh (follower) of yours."* Guru Jee welcomed Mansukh.

Guru Jee gave Bhia Mardana money and all the items for the wedding. Mardana happily went back to Talvandi. Mansukh's belief in Guru Jee grew in leaps and bounds. Two days later he requested Guru Jee, *"I am in your presence, please bless me."* Guru Jee said, *"Those people who are proud and entangled in selfish materialistic things, they experience a lot of pain and suffering in their lives. Without faith and belief in a True Guru they are not freed from the cycle of births and deaths. Hence leave behind your pride and attachments, lovingly meditate on the name of God (Vaaheguroo). Forget your ego and attach your mind to Vaaheguroo's name and live according to God's will. In this way you will obtain peace of mind."* Mansukh stayed in Sultanpur Lodhi serving Guru Jee for quite some time. Then he got permission to leave and returned home.

REVISION QUESTIONS
CHAPTER 10

1. Why did Bhai Mardana say he came to Sultanpur to see Guru Jee?
2. Where did Guru Jee send Bhagirath to purchase the items for the wedding from? Who did he bring back with him?
3. Why did Bhagirath refuse to stay the second night with the shopkeeper?
4. When Bhagirath and Mansukh came from Lahore to Guru Jee, what did Guru Jee say?
5. How did Guru Jee say Mansukh could obtain true happiness?

Chapter 11
GURU JEE GOES TO SACHKAND (Region of Truth)

One day Guru Jee said to Bhai Bala, *"I need to free myself from the affairs of the world and do some other work. You stay with Bebe Nanaki Jee."* He said to Bhagirath, *"You can go home now, but do return every now and again, to see us."*

One day Guru Jee went to the Stream (Bein) to bathe, just as He did every day and He was accompanied by a follower of His. Guru Jee brushed His teeth with the twig of a Jujube tree (a tree that bears a fruit called Ber) and once finished, buried the twig in the soil. At this place, there now stands a jujube tree which has grown from this twig that was buried (called Ber Sahib).

Guru Jee went into the stream to bathe, He took a full dip into the water, fully submerging His body under the water and then went to Sachkand (Region of Truth). The follower that was with Guru Jee stood at the bank of the stream holding Guru Jee's clothes. He waited and watched for ages, and when Guru Jee did not return out of the water, the follower got very worried and sad. He went to inform Daulat Khan of what had happened. He said, *"Guru Jee went to bathe in the stream this morning and took a full dip in the water and did not resurface."*

As soon as Daulat Khan heard this, he got onto his horse and hurried to the stream. He called a lot of boatmen and fishermen to come to help search for Guru Jee in the stream. Rumours quickly spread around the city that Daulat Khan's storekeeper has drowned in the stream. As news got to Jai Ram he was very worried and saddened, he also rushed to the stream. Everyone started to search for Guru Jee, but their searches were to no avail, everyone was very depressed and saddened to not find Guru Jee. Daulat Khan said, *"I will never find a storekeeper as good as him."*

Unlike everyone else, Bebe Nanaki was the only person who did not lose faith or hope. Bebe Nanaki said, *"My brother is the messenger of God, He is performing one of His miracles."* Then turning to her husband Jai Ram she said, *"Be patient and do not lose hope or become sad."* Thinking about what his wife, Jai Ram said, *"The fishermen and boatmen have dropped big nets into the water and have only been able to find and capture fish and water creatures. There is no sign of Guru Jee in the water."* Daulat Khan and his men were also walking around, looking dejected and hopeless.

Guru Jee's wife Mata Sulakhani, was very upset and crying a lot, grieving the loss of her husband. Bebe Nanaki was trying to comfort her and give her hope and said, *"You have not known my brother long and have not recognised His true identity. Why are you worrying and crying for no reason? Your husband will come back to you very soon. Believe and have faith in what I am telling you."* In this way Bebe Nanaki Jee kept reassuring and comforting the whole family and encouraging them, to remain strong and keep their faith in Guru Jee. Some people were praising Guru Jee while others were talking ill of them. As night fell, Bebe Nanaki attached her mind and thoughts to Guru Jee and prayed, *"Oh destroyer of all evil! Son of God! If the faith and belief I hold in you is true, then return to us and irradicate every ones' sadness."* In this way she spent the whole night meditating and requesting Guru Jee to keep the honour of the faith she held in Him.

When Guru Jee went to Sachkhand (Region of Truth), God lovingly addressed him by saying, *"Come dear Nanak, lover of my name! You have been sent to earth to teach people to believe and have faith in God, how much of this work have you done?"* Guru Jee replied, *"Our perfect Lord God! Where you have blessed me, I have tried*

Ber Sahib
The jujube tree which has grown from the twig Guru Jee planted

The stream where Guru Jee went to Sachkand

to get people to meditate upon your true name and I will continue to do so. In the future I will do as you command. The people of the world, hold faith in a living Guru first and then the Guru preaches to them and guides them. So please command me with what you want me to do."

Then to complete the discipline or teachings, God took the form of a Guru and bestowed the blessings of Mool Mantar as follows (this is the translation of the Mool Mantar, please take time out to read the Gurmukhi version or Romanized version, if you do not know what it is, it is the opening verse of Sri Guru Granth Sahib Jee):

The One God is the creator.
Truth is His Name.
 He is the doer of all that is manifest.
He is without fear.
He is without enemies.
His form is timeless.
He is beyond births and deaths.
He is Self-Existent.
He is realised by the grace of the Guru.

Then God said to Guru Jee, *"I want you to complete this Mool Mantar."* Guru Jee obeying God's wishes uttered,

Meditate on His Name.
He was true before the ages.
He is true at the start of the ages.
He is true now.
Sri Guru Nanak Dev Jee says, He shall be true in the future.

God was very pleased and said, *"All that recite this Mool Mantar, their pains and anguishes will be eradicated."* Then God instructed Guru Jee to give up His job as a storekeeper and to get the people of

Gurdwara Sant Ghat

This is on the banks of the stream, it marks the spot where Guru Jee re-appeared after going to Sachhand.

the world to meditate on the name of God, in order to free them from committing sins and realizing God. Then Guru Jee bid farewell to God and returned to Sultanpur.

Bebe Nanaki Jee used to send a follower of Guru Jee with Guru Jee's clothes to the river bank everyday. Three days later, early in the morning Guru Jee emerged from the water about a kilometre from the place where he had taken a dip and vanised into the stream. Today there is a Gurdwara at this place known as Sant Ghat Sahib.

The follower was standing at the river bank holding Guru Jee's clothes. On seeing him Guru Jee said, *"Oh Sikh become free from sufferings of the world."* Upon hearing these words the Sikhs' ignorance was eradicated and he was enlightened. Eventually Guru Jee arrived at Sultanpur Lodhi. He then sent the follower ahead of him and said, *"Go! Wherever my sister Nanaki is sitting meditating on God, I want you to respectfully bow down on the floor at her feet for me."*

Doing as he was told the Sikh hurried to Bebe Nanaki, she was at home and sitting in meditation when he arrived. The Sikh bowed down at her feet as he had been told to do and said, *"Your brother is coming."*

On hearing these words Bebe Nanaki opened her eyes and in sheer happiness and excitement went to Jai Ram and said, *"Dear husband, my brother is coming. Stop worrying now."* Upon seeing Guru Jee approaching, both Bebe Nanaki Jee and Jai Ram, went running to greet Guru Jee with devotion and the whole family followed.

The news of Guru Jee's return spread quickly around the whole village. Whoever heard about the news, came rushing to meet Guru Jee. Guru Jee gradually went and stood outside the store where He worked. He gave blessings to all the followers who came to

Inside Gurdwara Sant Ghat Sahib, an image showing Sri Guru Granth Sahib - the present Sikh Guru.

see Him. On seeing the doors of the store locked, Guru Jee asked, *"Who has closed this store?"* The Sikhs replied, *"Daulat Khan came himself and locked and sealed the store."* Guru Jee opened the doors to the store and said to the poor people, *"Whoever needs or wants anything, can take it from the store, without any fear of anyone."* The store was immediately bombarded by herds of poor people frantically taking things. This rush continued unabated for a long time, but the store did not fall low on any provisions even though people were taking out so much.

Somebody went and informed Daulat Khan about his store being open for the poor and needy to take provisions, under the guidance of Guru Jee. Daulat Khan was very shocked at hearing this and sent a servant of his to go and close down the store. He then went to see Guru Jee in person. Guru Jee was dressed in simple saintly attire. Seeing this saddened Daulat Khan and he said, *"Staying in the water for three days what evil spirit has possessed Him, He has got the whole of my store looted. He has become a holy man."* Seeing this he was saddened and he returned to his home immediately.

Guru Jee then went and sat in the middle of the cremation grounds. Some of the people of the city started to say, *"He has gone mad."* Some people went to Daulat Khan with the gossip about Guru Jee. They said Guru Jee has wasted and lost all your wealth, and used this as an excuse to become a holy man. They started to say to Daulat Khan, *"You should now check the store accounts and have them settled with Jai Ram as he was the storekeeper's referee."* Daulat Khan then called Jai Ram and said, *"Whatever losses I have suffered due to your brother-in-law I want you to pay back. If we are in negative figures you must repay the loss from your home."* Jai Ram then said, *"Let me go and meet Guru Jee at once, then I will come and settle your accounts."* Then Jai Ram went to Guru

Jee and respectfully said, *"Daulat Khan has asked me to settle his accounts for the last year."*

Guru Jee got up and went with Jai Ram to see Daulat Khan. Daulat Khan instructed the accountant to check all the accounts and figures for the past year. The accountant discovered that Guru Jee was in profit by 760 rupees. Jai ram was very happy. The accountant told Daulat Khan about what he had found. This surprised Daulat Khan and all the people who had gossiped and said bad things about Guru Jee's character were left feeling ashamed and embarrassed. Daulat Khan said to Guru Jee, *"Take what you are owed from me and I will also give you extra money to continue running the store for me."* Guru Jee said, *"I do not want the money, whatever money you owe me, I would rather you honestly distribute to the poor holy men."* After this Guru Jee returned to the cremation grounds and continued to pray. Bebe Nanaki's faith in Guru Jee was unmoved. She said, *"Whatever my Brother is doing is right, we have no right to say anything to Him."*

REVISION QUESTIONS
CHAPTER 11

1. When Daulat Khan was told that Guru Jee had not returned from the river what did he do?
2. Who had complete faith in Guru Jee being the messenger of God?
3. What did God say when Guru Jee was in Sachkhand?
4. When Guru Jee returned from the stream what did he do at the store?
5. What did Daulat Khan say to Jai Ram and what reply did Jai Ram give?
6. When the accounts for the year were checked how many rupees was Guru Jee owed?

Chapter 12
SRI GURU NANAK DEV JEE'S MARRIAGE

Guru Jee was engaged to Mata Sulakhani Jee. Their wedding was on Monday 19th May 1488 at Batala. His father in-laws' name was Moolchand Jee and His mother in-laws' name was Chando Rani Jee.

Guru Jee's marriage party went from Sultanpur Lodhi to Batala where they were lavishly welcomed. There was an unstable wall there. Moolchand's priest prepared the holy fire place where the couple were to walk around for the marriage ceremony. The priest told Guru Jee to walk around the fire.

Guru Jee said, *"I do not hold faith or belief in the fire and will not walk around it."* The priest said to Moolchand, *"Your son in law is not listening to us. If you say we will try to make him understand and listen."* The Brahmins (priests) got Moolchands agreement, and everyone tried very hard to get Guru Jee to obey the priests, and carry out the wedding in the way that they were requesting. Guru Jee said, *"Our belief and faith is in Akaal Purakh (Immortal God). I will not walk around or circle anything or any person except for God or God's name."* Hence Guru Jee did not agree to perform the wedding around the fire and the priests' then took on a more stubborn attitude. They all made a plan and decided that they would make the unstable wall fall onto Guru Jee, to instill some fear into Guru Jee, they thought Guru Jee will then listen to us. They made Guru Jee get very close to the unstable wall.

Guru Jee was fearless and nothing could scare Him. An elderly woman overheard the priests talking about this plan of theirs. She said to Guru Jee, *"This wall is about to fall, get up and move from*

Gurdwara Kandh Sahib
The unstable wall is inside this Gurdwara

here." On the blind side of the wall some of the priests men started to demolish the wall. Guru Jee said, *"Mother, do not fear. This wall will not fall. It will remain as a momento of my wedding for years to come."* When Guru Jee said these words the wall stood as it was and did not fall. Then not a single one of the tricks that the priests plotted worked.

When all the priests attempts failed, then one priest named Hardiyal said, *"You are the King of millions of universes and are our guest, I am your priest. You had blessed me with the knowledge of the holy thread (Hindu ritualistic thread, Janeeo), please now in the same way, tell me the way in which a marriage ceremony should be performed. What will you walk around or circle to take your marriage vows?"* Guru Jee said, *"We will walk around the name of God."* At that time Guru Jee requested a paper, quill and ink and a wooden stand, and with their own hands wrote the Mool Mantar on the piece of paper;

The One God is the creator.
Truth is His Name.
He is the doer of all that is manifest.
He is without fear.
He is without enemies.
His form is timeless.
He is beyond births and deaths.
He is Self-Existent.
He is realised by the grace of the Guru.
Meditate on His Name.
He was true before the ages.
He is true at the start of the ages.
He is true now.
Sri Guru Nanak Dev Jee says, He shall be true in the future.

Guru Jee covered the wooden stand with a clean piece of cloth and

ਜਿਸ ਵਕਤ ਸ੍ਰੀ ਗੁਰੂ ਨਾਨਕ ਦੇਵ ਜੀ ਵਲਾਇਤ ਵਲਿਓਂ ਵਿਚਰਦੇ ਗਏ ਕਾਇਨਾਤ ਵੱਲ ਜਾਂਦੇ ਹੋਏ ਰਾਹ ਵਿਚ.....
ਇਕ ਸਾਧੂ ਨੇ ਗੁਰੂ ਜੀ ਨੂੰ ਮਿਲ ਕੇ ਕਿ ਆਪ ਵੀ ਵਿਚ ਵੱਡੇ ਧੰਨੀ ਹੋ ਅਤੇ ਬਾਹਰ ਵਾਲੀ ਹੈ ..ਤੇ ਇਸ ਤੋਂ ਦੇ
ਪਤੇ ਦੇ ਜਾ—ਤਾਂ ਗੁਰੂ ਜੀ ਨੇ ਆਖਿਆ....ਭਾਈ ਤੂੰ ਉਚਾਰ ਇਹਦ ਜੋ ਹੁੰਦੀ ਜੂ ਨਾਰਾਇਣ ਸਰੂਪ ਅਤੇ ਵੇਦਕੀ
ਸਾਰੇ ਵਿਖਿਆਰ ਦੀ ਜਾਦਾ ਰਾਮ ਹੁੰਦੇ ਜੀ ਹੈ॥   .....

placed the piece of paper with the Mool Mantar on it, on the stand. Guru Jee then along with their bride walked four times around the Mool Mantar, then they both respectfully bowed down on the floor in front of the Mool Mantar. Guru Jee had set a new tradition that Sikhs only walk around Gurbani (the Guru's hymns) when getting married and do not walk around a fire. The Fourth Guru, Sri Guru Ram Das Jee uttered the four Lavan or hymns of bliss, that are sung to conduct the wedding ceremony. The Fifth Guru, Sri Guru Arjan Dev Jee compiled the bani from the first four Guru Sahibs as well as their own Bani and got Bhai Gurdas Jee to scribe the Sri Guru Granth Sahib Jee. From then on Sri Guru Arjan Dev Jee introduced the tradition that marriages are to be conducted, by the marital couple walking around Sri Guru Granth Sahib Jee.

The groom's wedding party stayed in Batala for three days, and on the fourth day Baba Kalu Jee bid farewell to Moolchand Jee and the wedding party returned to Sultanpur. At the place of that unstable wall there is now a beautiful Gurdwara called Kandh (wall) Sahib. A part of the wall is still standing within a glass display cabinet within the Gurdwara.

The place where Guru Jee's marriage ceremony took place is a little distance from the wall, at the place where Moolchand's house was, a Gurdwara named Dera Sahib now stands there.

REVISION QUESTIONS
CHAPTER 12

1. Where and when did Guru Nanak Dev Jee's marriage take place?
2. What did Moolchand's priest ask Guru Jee to do and what was Guru Jee's reply?
3. What request did Hardiyal, the priest make to Guru Jee?
4. What tradition did the Fifth Guru Sahib start?

Platform
This is where the Mool Mantar was placed and Guru Jee & Mata Sulakhni walked around it to get married.

Chapter 13
GURU JEE WENT TO THE MOSQUE

A few days passed with Guru Jee sitting and praying in the cremation grounds. Then Guru Jee's father-in-law went to the governor and said, *"The 760 rupees that your storekeeper is owed should be given to His family."* Daulat Khan said, *"He has asked me to distribute the 760 rupees amongst the poor holy men, so we should call Him and ask Him first."* Daulat Khan then sent one of his men to call Guru Jee, but Guru Jee did not come. On hearing this Daulat Khan was very angry and said, *"If He doesn't come of his own accord arrest Him and make Him come."* The man then returned to Guru Jee and told Him what the Nawab had said. In order to break Daulat Khan's pride Guru Jee came but did not greet Daulat Khan.

The Nawab said, *"Why did you not come, when I first asked you to?"* Guru Jee replied, *"When I was your servant, I came to you on your calling. Now I am not your servant. I am now the servant of God. That's why I didn't come."* The Kazi (Muslim priest) said, *"If you are a man of God, then God sees Muslims and Hindus as one. If you also see everyone as equal, then come with us to the mosque to pray with us."* Guru Jee replied *"Ok, let's go."*

The governor and Kazi started towards the mosque to pray with Guru Jee. As people heard about this they rushed to the mosque and soon the mosque became very crowded. Jai Ram heard what was happening and was very upset and said, *"Today Nanak Jee will read the Namaz(Muslim prayer) and become a muslim. This is a very bad thing."* Bebe Nanaki Jee said, *"My brother is the messenger of God. He will defeat those people and return. Stop being afraid. If you don't believe me, send someone to go and find out what is happening."* Jai Ram sent a Brahmin (Hindu priest) to go and find out what was happening. Due to the big crowds gathered at the mosque, the Brahmin could not get close to Guru Jee and had to stay a little distance away.

The governor and the Kazi started to read the Namaz and Guru Jee remained standing still. Once the two of them had completed the Namaz they said, *"Why did you not do the Namaz with us?"*

Guru Jee said, *"Who should I have done Namaz with?*

The governor answered, *"You should have done it with me."*

Guru Jee said, *"You were not doing the Namaz. You were saying the words of the namaz from your mouth and ritualistically doing the actions of the Namaz, but your mind and thoughts were very far away. Your mind was busy buying horses from Kabul."*

The Kazi then said, *"Why are you not afraid, when speaking lies?"*

The governor said, *"He is right, my mind was in Kabul buying horses."*

The Kazi said, *"Then you should have done Namaz with me."*

Guru Jee replied, *"Your mind was also not here, you have had a mare give birth at your house and you were afraid that the baby mare may fall and drown in the well. Your mind running around after the baby mare."*

The Kazi said, *"You are right this is what happened."*

On hearing this surprising revelation, people started to laugh. The governor then bowed and respectfully touched Guru Jee's feet said, *"You are the saint of saints, I am in your sanctuary, I was a lost person and did not recognize your true identity. Please forgive me for my ignorance and mistakes. Give me your blessings. You are the form of God Himself and are all knowing. You have been living near me for so long and I never knew your greatness. My mind is not within my control it wanders here and there, please bless me so that I am able to control it."*

Guru Jee said, *"The mind wanders a lot, it is very difficult to control. Without stopping it from wondering we cannot feel the true love of God within ourselves. This mind can only be controlled on meeting with the true and perfect Guru. So meditate on God's name and bring it under control."* Daulat Khan enshrined these words of Guru Jee within his heart and with both hands together respectfully bowed down in front of Guru Jee and said, *"From this day on I am your Sikh (follower)."*

Guru Jee said, *"Apart from the true name of God almighty, all else in this world is false. A prayer is only a true prayer, if the mind is detached from this world and attached to God. Prayer is not just a ritualistic act or facade, done in order to show off in front of people."*

Daulat Khan said, *"Guru Jee the money of yours that I have, has been requested by your father-in-law. He has said that it should be given to him for your family. You have said to distribute it amongst the poor. What should I do with it?* Guru Jee said, *"Do as you feel is right. Nobody will stop you."* Daulat khan said, *"I will give half the money to your family and the other half to the poor saints."*

The Brahmin that Jai Ram had sent to find out about what was happening, came back and told him about everything he had heard and witnessed. Jai Ram was very happy after hearing all this. After some time passed Guru Jee also came to meet Bebe Nanaki and Jai Ram.

REVISION QUESTIONS
CHAPTER 13

1. How many rupees did Daulat Khan owe Guru Jee? Who did Guru Jee say the rupees should be given to?
2. What enlightened revelations did Guru Jee show everyone in the mosque?
3. How did Guru Jee say the mind can be controlled?
4. Who did Daulat Khan decide to give the money to?

Chapter 14
PURCHASING THE RABAB

Somebody went to Talvandi and informed Baba Kalu Jee that their son Nanak, had quit the job of storekeeper and has become a saint. On hearing this Baba Kalu Jee sent Bhai Mardana to Sultanpur Lodhi to check on Guru Jee. When Bhai Mardana arrived at Sultanpur Lodhi, Bebe Nanaki asked him about her parents well being. Bhai Mardana told her all about her parents being well and then told her the reason for his visit.

Bebe Nanaki said, *"If you want to know about everything that has happened, have some food to eat and then sit with brother, and ask Him all about it."*

Guru Jee was sitting in the forest. Bhai Mardana went and respectfully greeted Guru Jee and said, *"What have you become? The job of storekeeper was very good, why did you leave your job?"*

Guru Jee replied, *"Mardana I have to travel the country and globe. Some time ago you came and asked for some priceless gifts off me. I happily gave you the gift of how to play string instruments. Hence now I need your skills. Stay with me day and night, and don't even think of going any place else."*

Bhai Mardana said, *"Baba Kalu has sent me to check up on you. He will be waiting for me to return, and will be worried about you."*

Guru Jee replied, *"Do as you feel is right, by staying with me you will have to live through difficult and testing times. If you want an easy life of luxuries, then go to my father, live a happy and peaceful life with your family."*

Bhai Mardana pondered on what Guru Jee said to him and he made a decision, *"I have made a definite decision that I am going to stay with you Guru Jee."*

Guru Jee said, *"Go to the town and purchase a rabab(string instrument) to play."* Bhai Mardana said, *"Guru Jee! I have never played a rabab, but will learn how to play it in just a few days."*

Guru Jee said, *"We had bestowed the knowledge of a musician unto you. Where are those skills?"* Bhai Mardana replied, *"I have never tried to use the blessings you gave me, by trying to play an instrument."*

Guru Jee said, *"Don't refuse my request, go and purchase a rabab and come and play it."* Bhai Mardana hurried to town and said to a musician, *"A very sincere person is calling you, so get a rabab and come with me."*

The musician came to Guru Jee and played the rabab. Guru Jee was very pleased. Guru Jee said to Bhai Mardana, *"Now you play the rabab."*

Bhai Mardana took the rabab from the musician and started to play it. On hearing the melodious tune the musician was very surprised and said, *"I have never seen or heard such a skilled musician in my life."*

Guru Jee said to Bhai Mardana, *"How did you like playing the rabab?"* Bhai Mardana replied, *"You are the complete, perfect form of God, it was only with your words and grace, that I acquired this talent."*

Guru Jee said, *"Go to my sister and get money off her to purchase a rabab."* Bhai Mardana did as he was told and went to get money from Bebe Nanaki. During this time the musician said to Guru Jee, *"Maharaj Jee! Have this rabab".*

Guru Jee said, *"Your rabab has come to us. You keep it now."* Guru Jee then blessed the musician and dispelled all his pains and sufferings. Bhai Mardana said to Bebe Nanaki, *"Guru Jee has sent me to you to get money to buy a rabab."*

Bebe Nanaki said, *"It is a good thing that you have decided to stay with brother. What's one rabab, you can buy a hundred. Tell my brother to come and meet me."*

Bhai Mardana returned to Guru Jee and told him of Bebe Nanaki's request. Guru Jee said to Bhai Mardana, *"Sister is older than me, I cannot disobey her request."* Guru Jee then went to His sister's house. Bebe Nanaki put down a stool for Guru Jee to sit on. Guru Jee said, *"Dear sister! What purpose did you call me here for?"* Bebe Nanaki said, *"I was missing you and wanted to meet you."*

Guru Jee said, *"Whenever you think of me, no matter where I am I will come to you."* On hearing these words Bebe Nanaki was very happy. She then served food to everyone and said to Bhai Mardana, *"Take this money and go and purchase a rabab."* Bhai Mardana went to buy a rabab.

Bhai Bala said to Guru Jee, *"It has been a long time since I left home, may I now go and see how my house and family are?"* Guru Jee replied, *"Ask for whatever you want."*

Bhai Bala said, *"Grant me the boon that Gods name dwells within me forever and that I never become doubtful or unfaithful."* Guru Jee said, *"This wish of yours will be granted."* Bhai Bala then respectfully bowed at Guru Jee's feet and returned home.

Meanwhile Bhai Mardana searched everywhere for a rabab. Nobody spoke to him with any respect or courtesy. People said things like, *"He is the lost wanderer's musician."* Bhai Mardana returned to Guru Jee and told him of what happened.

Guru Jee once again told him to go and buy a rabab. Bhai Mardana said, *"You are all knowing. Where should I go to get the rabab from?* Guru Jee said, *"Towards the north, where two rivers meet, in between them is a village. Ask for a musician named Farinda and get the rabab from him. If he refuses to give you the rabab mention my name and say that I have sent you."*

Bhai Mardana then left to get the rabab. When he got there he asked many people about a person named Farinda but nobody knew of him. He was very tired and sad and decided to rest under a tree for a while. A man came and asked, *"Who are you looking for and where have you come from? What is your name? Tell me."*

Bhai Mardana replied, *"Sri Guru Nanak Dev Jee has sent me to look for a musician named Farinda to purchase a rabab from. I have searched for him for days but have not yet found him"*. The man then said, *"I am Farinda. Guru Jee has sent you to me. Take this rabab from me."*

Then he suddenly got a rabab from somewhere and gave it to Bhai Mardana. Bhai Mardana was very happy and surprised at receiving the rabab and said, *"What is the price of this rabab?"* Bhai Farinda replied, *"You do not have how much it is worth. I don't want it's worth either."*

Bhai Mardana then said, *"How are you gifting this rabab to me, and not taking it's worth from me. Tell me the reason behind this and put my curiosity to rest."* Bhai Farinda said, *"Do not think of this rabab as being from this universe. Do not play this rabab in front of anyone accept Sri Guru Nanak Dev Jee. You must only play it for Guru Jee. I will go with you."*

On reaching where Guru Jee was, the two of them bowed down in front of Guru Jee. It was on the ninth day that Bhai Mardana returned with the rabab. Guru Jee said to Bhai Mardana, *"You have taken so many days in returning. What happened?"* Bhai Mardana replied, *"You know everything, it took me three days to get there, then three days to find Bhai Farinda and then another three days coming back."*

Bhai Farinda said, *"I had the desire to meet you and give the rabab to you. I am now very happy after having met you. You are enlightened and know everything."*

He then started to leave. Guru Jee sent Bhai Mardana to see him off. After a little distance he vanished. Bhai Mardana was very shocked at seeing this.upon his return Guru Jee enquired, *"Bhai Mardana! Where did you see him off till?"*

Bhai Mardana said, *"After a short distance he vanished and I could not see him. Guru Jee! Who was that man?"* Guru Jee said, *"He was a saint from the nether regions (afterlife). He worships and meditates on God with a lot of love and devotion. He had the desire to gift this rabab to me for a long time. Now play the rabab."*

When Bhai Mardana played the rabab; the melody that sounded from it was "YOU ARE GREAT, OH ALL PERVASIVE GOD, YOU ARE GREAT, OH GOD." On hearing this, Guru Jee remained in deep meditation for two days. On the third day he awoke from this meditation.

REVISION QUESTIONS
CHAPTER 14

1. Why did Baba Kalu send Bhai Mardana to Guru Jee?
2. Where and to whom did Guru Jee send Bhai Mardana to get the rabab from?
3. When Bebe Nanaki missed Guru Jee what did Guru Jee say to her?
4. What did Bhai Farinda say to Bhai Mardana?
5. What did Guru Jee tell Bhai Mardana about Bhai Farinda?

To be continued …

Please purchase
The Great Guru Nanak, Vol. 2,
When released.

Please check www.akaalpublishers.com
for updates on progress

Delivering Timeless Messages

www.akaalpublishers.com